Come
Home
to
Happiness

Come Home to Happiness

Sharon Hoffman

New Leaf Press

First printing: January 1999

ISBN: 0-89221-472-4
Library of Congress Number: 99-070073

Cover by Janell Robertson
Cover art by Kit Hevron Mahoney

Printed in the United States of America.

Dedication

To my mother
Lindy Baird
in whose heart and home I find sweet
comfort!

Thank you.

Blessed be God. . . . Who comforteth us in all our tribulation, that we may be able to comfort them which are in any trouble, by the comfort wherewith we ourselves are comforted of God (2 Cor. 1:3-4).

Acknowledgments

My heart holds dear all the precious ones in my life who have helped to make these pages a reality . . . many thanks from my heart go out:

To my husband, Rob, for giving me daily gifts of love, encouragement, and perspective. The greatest comfort in my life is having you by my side!

To Mindy, Missy, and Mike — how grateful I am to be your mom. You three bring chaos and comfort to my life . . . I love both!

To Dana Grimes for your polished writing contribution, and especially for your sustaining prayer, perseverance, and *pushing*. (You always seem to know when I need the latter!)

To my dear CCBC gals for carving out periods of quiet for me and for being an awesome "test group" for much of this material. Your lives verify God's comfort!

To the New Leaf Press family! You heard my passion and have been great each step of this project. I'm grateful to partner with such a godly, fun-loving team.

To Florence Littauer for your enthusiasm right from the start! You and Marita truly *wanted* me to write this series. You're the best!

To Marabel Morgan, whose teachings when I was just a newly-wed spawned much of my learning for loving my husband and my home.

And to you, dear reader friend, may God truly be the comfort of your heart and of your home.

Introduction

Welcome! I'd love to invite you into my home through the pages of this book. One of the greatest benefits of my having a home office nowadays is the flexibility to do just that. I always welcome the break that a spontaneous visit with a friend affords.

Make yourself right at home. Go right ahead and snuggle back into the plump pillows on our sofa. That's what they're there for. Linger awhile. We'll share a cup of tea, cocoa, coffee — your choice. Feel free to get cozy as we share these moments in close companionship. I hope you will feel the laid-back coziness that my family and I take pleasure in whenever we're at home. We want you to feel it, too.

If you are like the friends I have met in recent months through an avalanche of correspondence in my travels crisscrossing the country, we have much in common. I have laughed with a newlywed in Florida, cried with divorcees in Massachusetts and California, and prayed with a newly widowed young mother of three in the Philippines. You know what I've found? I find, indeed, that the number one common denominator among women in every corner of the planet is the precious place we call *home*.

Everywhere, at all ages and every status of life, women place high priority on nurturing a home of happiness. These pages are lovingly composed to help you discover ideas that can transform your home into a place of comfort. You may be surprised when you find where we'll start. More surprises will follow when you discover where touring through our homes will take us!

Maybe your house is ready for some home improvement projects. Let's look at your home in some new and exciting ways. You may live in humble quarters of a rented, shared room. Perhaps where you call home is a spacious suburban ranch, maybe a sprawling three-story Victorian manor, or an itty-bitty country cottage. Wherever you call home, if you want your home to survive . . . and yes, thrive, then this book is for you!

You may be thinking, *My home doesn't have a prayer*. If so, I encourage you to stay with me a little longer. I've seen some remarkable turnarounds! Read on. I urge you to make another try! Every house (and the people living in it) need a few home improvement projects from time to time. Remember, "Rome wasn't built in a day." And neither is a home!

Before you knock down a wall . . . tear up a bath . . . replace one window . . . or start planning an addition, join me in getting started with the right tools and materials. These basic but beautiful re-decorating principles will not only put comfort into your home, but they promise a happiness in your heart!

Come Home to Happiness

Entering a Home of Joy

By the time my husband, Rob, and I made the down payment on our home 11 years ago, I had lived in about as many houses as I was years old. When I was a child and throughout my first few years of marriage, we moved often. A home of my own represented a "putting down of roots" — which would be an important element in my quest for personal comfort and stability.

The moment our realtor and I first stepped inside our home-to-be, how my heart sank! Walking through each room confirmed the harsh reality of what I'd suspected from the outside. The whole house was in dire need of *major* repair and remodeling. Yet the minute I walked through the door, I knew somehow we could make this ours. So we have! I chattered non-stop the rest of the evening about ways *I just knew* this house could be turned into a home, regardless of the gruesome greeting we'd just received.

With a lot of help from friends and good old-fashioned elbow grease, the endeavor began. The challenge we faced included stained linoleum floors, bathrooms that leaked, and a deck so rotted that one day while I was pacing and talking on the phone, I fell through . . . right up to my waist!

As many as five multiple layers of former floor coverings and/or wallpaper had to be removed in many of the rooms! Every room was dark with depressingly somber paint or covered with cracked mirror squares (removal left half of us wounded!).

After an enormous amount of work the home began to come alive! Yours can, too! Looking through the eyes of potential made our creative process possible. My ever-optimistic outlook helped us envision a place that eventually stopped requiring daily repair. Increasingly, laughter and family spirit replaced the long hours of labor. Love transformed our house into a home. Creating a home of comfort is an attitude that opens us up to endless possibilities.

Yes, I know our furnishings, carpets, and walls will someday fade. The kitchen will cease feeding hungry souls. Music and laughter will no longer fill our rooms. But, precious memories of family and fellowship will live on forever in our hearts. That's the primary reason I want to inspire you and give you hope for your own home!

Let's go on a home re-decorating adventure. Let the spirit of comfort begin in your own life . . . first in your own heart and attitudes. It will spill over onto everyone else in your home. You don't need to be torn down, bulldozed away, and re-built from the ground up. A comforting home is not so much *finding* the right house as *being the right person inside that house.* Most women I know would like to improve their homes, but are concerned with the things they *do.* The role of a soothing, softening woman is something you *are.* That gets us down to basic interior decorating.

Blueprints for Blessedness

When I mentioned that in a seminar recently, one woman winced and said, "If comfort starts on the inside, I've got a *lot* of interior decorating to do. Looks like I'll be busy a while." She was right. Re-decorating our attitude does take work, but the results are well worth it! If I'm ever going to create comfort in my home I must confront my own weaknesses and acknowledge vulnerable places in my own heart.

Our houses are the outward expression of our true home — that "real you" which is inside of each person. Thus, you can never put heart and soul into a house if it is not first inside you. That's what makes *your* house uniquely yours since our houses take on each owner's personality. If anger, bitterness, and strife are the condition of your heart it makes sense that your household will take on those qualities.

If a real estate agent wanted to do a write-up on your house, what would its description say? Far beyond the physical description of your home, how would you describe the emotional environment, ambiance, and spiritual temperature? If you and I want to creatively adorn our homes, let's begin with the entrance. Upon entering, others will be inspired to spend time in your home as they are welcomed with a pleasing reception.

You have the power to lift your family's spirits or bring them down to rock bottom. I can guarantee that if you make your family's entrances a welcoming experience, they will be eager to head home often! Knowing they will enter into a shelter from the storms of life brings great comfort. We all need to take sanctuary behind doors where caring arms await to hug and hold.

A friend of mine shared an epitaph she had seen while walking through a park and adjoining cemetery. The inscription read: SHE WAS THE SUNSHINE OF OUR HOME. Donna said the rest of her walk she kept thinking, *That's probably the last thing they'd put on my tombstone.* She determined that afternoon to be pleasant even if her house was in chaos when she returned!

You can become the sunshine in your home, but first you must learn where the clouds are. The first four minutes after arrival into the home are critical in setting the tone for the rest of the evening. If you are cheery and comforting tonight, chances are your husband and children will be. If you are gripey and growly, they probably will be too, since they take their cues from you.

Homecoming Hugs

At our house, coming home is something to celebrate! We place a high premium on respect for one another so we welcome each other home with enthusiasm. When we hear that garage door opening, it is our signal to welcome one another home

Hugs are the best form of emotional and physical therapy.

eagerly. It communicates, "You were missed! I'm so glad you're home!"

I make every effort to hug each family member as they walk through our door. No, it may not always be convenient to stop what I'm doing, but I do anyway. Tender touches are ways to communicate my expressions of love. Try it — for some it will be awkward at first. It will come easier to you the more you do it. Your family will love it. What a shame that many children (adults, too) will pillow their head tonight without one hug or satisfying touch from a loved one all day long.

Everyone you live with will live a happier, healthier life from experiencing frequent touches. Scientific results indicate many emotional and health benefits from at least 8 to 12 touches a day. Fluffy animals are brought in for hospital and nursing home residents to caress and hug. It makes their day! "Hugs are the best form of emotional and physical therapy," reports Jo Lindberg, founder of the Hugs for Health Foundation.

Touch comforts. Touching gives a sense of safety and security, no matter what our age. Infants thrive when held by humans who care for them. A gentle, soothing touch upon returning home, at bedtime, and for "no reason at all" wraps us in a warm security blanket of comfort. It reassures of love, acceptance, and that *"everything's gonna be alright"* feeling.

Sometimes I may choose to pout and withdraw with a "poor me" pity party for myself. Giving in to my gripey attitude (and starting the day by slinging cereal bowls across the table) only multiplies the problem. It does not take long and we have more than one Oscar the Grouch at the breakfast table!

Things seem to start off much better when I determine to set a positive attitude first thing in the morning. In the mornings when I awake, before I crawl out of bed, I thank the God for another day and for what it will bring. Maybe I'm to clean house that day, or travel, or work in my office or meet a friend for coffee. The day's schedule is not the issue . . . my heart attitude is. "This is the day the Lord has made; let us rejoice and be glad in it" (Ps. 118:24). I have a choice to rejoice! And so do you.

Comfort Is Contagious

What is your attitude toward day-to-day life? Do you know that your personal happiness depends on the attitude you will have? It does. It's deeper than the "full cup, empty cup" outlook. It is essential that we see ourselves in light of God's true Word . . . then be open to change when change is needed.

"But, nobody's perfect."

"That's just the way I am."

"I was born this way."

"If you only knew what I've been through."

"It's not my fault."

Excuses come so easily. Maybe you return home exhausted. Maybe your husband opens the front door upset and wants to pick a fight. Out of your own resources of love and by an act of your will, you can *choose* to be a blessing rather than a burden!

I know. I've had to myself. I had to just last night.

Mile-long Rooftops

During Bible days, apartment-type homes were built in and on top of the city walls. To protect the home from sun and rain, part of the roof extended beyond the walls. The word describing the overhang is "forbear," which means an "outroof." The same word is used in the command to forbear one another in love (see Eph. 4:2-3). God is telling us to outroof one another *in love*.

I had to *choose* to be a blessing of comfort in our home by "outroofing" (protecting) Rob from his fatigue after he returned home last night exhausted. He did not know how to get off the merry-go-round he had been on all week after a hectic holiday calendar of parties, appointments, and meetings. I lovingly chose to withdraw from last night's events when I realized the stress within Rob.

Sure, I wanted to go to the event . . . I was not "peopled out" since I'd been in my office alone most of the workday. But, it was just another way of saying, "I don't always have to have my way. You are important." *Choose* to go the extra mile. It really pays off! Being comforted after his stressful day, Rob then renewed and filled our home with kindness and laughter as we chatted through the evening. I believe my determination to be a blessing, not a burden, was a good choice.

Learn to Laugh

One of the most soothing sounds you can hear upon entering your own home is laughter coming from those you love. What a lift to any heavy heart who steps inside! As we learn to bring humor into our lives, we are relaxed and put at ease.

Laughing at yourself is great therapy for any tense situation. Our Mindy recently offered to prepare a special chicken dinner for Rob and me. I got home later than usual from an appointment to hear

One of the most soothing sounds you can hear upon entering your own home is laughter coming from those you love.

wails of hysteria from the kitchen. Watching to see my reaction to a huge mess upon my arrival, Mindy proceeded to describe the steps of her culinary efforts . . . and how the kitchen arrived in its present state of shambles.

Mindy's description of her clumsiness while pouring from a slippery pitcher, egg shells that wouldn't crack, and how her right hand had gotten lodged between the oven rack and cake pan were hilarious. We survived the ordeal by pitching in together for the cleanup. The more questions I asked about "How did this get *here?*" the harder we laughed.

Rob returned a half an hour later to find us both slumped into chairs, laughing to the point of tears. He said he could hear the laughter all the way from the driveway and couldn't wait to get inside! I got to hear the scenario all over again! Then, we all pitched in to be a part of the hazardous waste cleanup crew!

Laughter Comforts

The more you look for humor in life, the more you find it. Some days are so devastating you have to look pretty hard. Solomon knew what he was talking about when he said, "A cheerful heart is good medicine" (Prov. 17:22). Rob received a tonic that day when he arrived home.

Doctors agree that everyone needs to laugh more. In several Mayo

Clinic Health Letters experts have reported that laughter is a wonderful antidote in curing depressing health and emotional problems. Learn to chuckle at situations that are ridiculous — it helps put your problems into perspective. And it sure is fun to return home to!

Barbara Johnson, author and humorist, says to remember:

> Laughter is like changing a baby's diaper: It doesn't permanently solve any problems, but it makes things more acceptable for a while.

Let the Light Shine Through

Smiles are a delight to come home to! Acquire the habit of smiling. Few people realize the value and power a smile can give to others! When you give a smile, you transfer attention from yourself to others. It communicates, "I'm here for you," not "What can you do for me?" Thus, your own health, joy, and self-esteem is strengthened.

The more you look for humor in life, the more you find it.

Women who radiate true, timeless beauty know that secret! A smile is the outward evidence of inward joy and praise which brings glory to God. I have traveled to countries where language posed a barrier, but have never had trouble communicating if I wore a smile! Somehow, it communicates worth and encouragement in a very practical sense.

Regardless of how you feel on the inside (feelings are so fickle), learn that a smile is so important in having an abiding joy. Jesus calls it, "the abundant life." He himself designed the perfect house plans when He said, "If you remain in me and my words remain in you, ask whatever you wish, and it will be given you. . . . Ask and you will receive, and your joy will be complete" (John 15:7–16:24).

The condition for such joy is allowing Jesus to sit at the control center of your home. To relinquish those controls, you and I must depend on His sure Word of truth, no matter what comes. That's how I'll know I'm building according to His plan. It sure takes the pressure off of me. When I do take the controls back, I'm sorry I have. For I have "tasted" the abundant life and that's the kind of home I want. As King David expressed it long ago, "You have made known to me the path of life; you will fill me with joy in your presence" (Ps. 16:11).

As a light in the window beckons to those on the outside, "Someone's home, we invite you in," so a smile lights up your face giving those on the outside a message, "Love lives here. I'm here for you, I invite you into my heart." It's what I like to call a "yes" face instead of a "no" face. Approachable. Hopeful. It reaches out and touches others!

Where Seldom Is Heart a Discouraging Word

You may have seen the cartoon a few years ago, of a man sitting at the breakfast table reading his paper. His wife is sure he's not listening, but asks, "Are you listening to me?"

"Of course, dear," he replies without looking up.

Frustrated, she shouts, "The state inspector was here. He has condemned our house because it's being eaten by giant termites."

"Yes, dear," he replies.

Exasperated by this time, she slams down her coffee cup and stalks out of the room.

Women! Who can understand them? hubby thinks to himself, shaking his head.

Not only do some families need to smile a bit more, they need also to communicate a lot more as well. When the lines of communication are open with some "give and take" on *both* sides, there is hope for strong relationships between family

Ask and you will receive, and your joy will be complete

(John 16:24).

members. How do you keep these lines open? May I offer a few suggestions:

WARNING! DO NOT READ THIS BOOK —

Unless, of course, you want to learn, as I am learning, some vital issues about words and speech. James tells us that the tongue is like a bit in a horse's mouth; if we control the bit, we can control the whole horse. Since I am one who tends to speak before I think, I'm trying to learn to follow the general rule from the Bible: "Whatsoever things are true . . . honest . . . just . . . pure . . . lovely . . . of good report . . . think on these things" (Phil 4:8;KJV).

This admonition sounds slightly "Pollyanna," but it miraculously brings joy to my heart. If I deliberately think "on the good" I begin to feel more kindly toward Rob and other people, too. Then, I am not so likely to tear them down.

Negative cut-downs are huge communication barriers. No one likes to carry on a conversation with someone who is negative, cutting, and discouraging. In fact, we avoid people like that. Throughout our first year of marriage, I did not know that a man cannot communicate with a negative, nagging wife. *I* was making our communication break down.

When I discovered the biblical ethic of communicating in affirming, positive ways, Rob began to talk again. His and my needs were restored and esteem confirmed in both of us. Encouraging words are meaningful gifts that can say to a needy heart, "I love you!"

I love Paul's reminder to the Thessalonians when he said, "For you know that we dealt with each of you as a father deals with his own children" (1 Thess. 2:11). A loving father gently urges his children. He encourages. He is just and uplifting. His words build up; they do not tear down.

Even as I was writing those words, the doorbell rang, and I received a note from the hands of the small daughter of a neighbor friend. The note contained some dear words of encouragement that just made my day. After doing piles of laundry, cleaning the garage, and running errands, the encouragement came when it counted!

How vital are comforting, encouraging words! I recently had the privilege of spending a day with a well-known author. As I observed her life, I realized that she had developed and honed the gift of encouragement like no one I had ever seen. All day long I heard her encourage, thank, and ask insightful questions of those around her. Praise flowed naturally out of her mouth. Others wanted to be near her. She wasn't "putting on," she had literally made it a point to develop a good habit of saying encouraging words.

Proverbs tells us that the mouth of the righteous is a "fountain of life" (Prov. 10:11). I came away refreshed from being with that dear woman. Not because she's famous or an author, but, her speech filled so many thirsting hearts that day . . . mine included.

Stop! Look! Listen!

We women are often great at being preoccupied while family members are trying to talk with us. Filing our nails, talking on the phone, or thumbing through a magazine shows others disrespect and disinterest. However egotistical it may seem, each of us is delighted when another person really cares about what we are saying by *stopping* what they are doing . . . *looking* at us in the eye . . . and really *listening!*

You can put others at ease to converse — yes, even your teenagers — by finding questions designed to "draw out" the other person. By taking time out to stop what you are doing, you are creating an immediate rapport with those in your home. That's how we learn about each other . . . to really know and love each other.

Many suburban homes are silent except for the sounds of the CD player blaring, a high-speed modem punching away to download a memo, and the racket of three phone lines so tied up that Dad can't get on the web to check his e-mail. Families are spending more time communicating with electronics than with each other.

One family related to me, "Each time we come home, we each go directly to the computer, phone answering machine, or stereo. Buttons and knobs are being pushed in every room of the house. A whole evening can go by without any interaction with whoever else is in the house." Beep, beep, ring, ring, da, da, da. . . . How sad, but probably true in far too many homes.

The hum of a spiritless technological security blanket does not comfort like the soft, articulate utterance of a hug, compliment, or encouraging word.

Open House, Open Heart

The moment folks step up to your door, they are getting a glimpse of what is inside. We want our home to have an atmosphere that draws others to us . . . to open up ourselves rather than to shut others out. There are many little touches that can

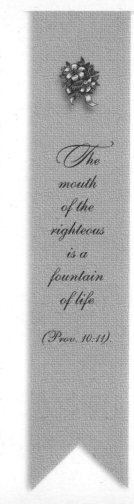

The mouth of the righteous is a fountain of life

(Prov. 10:11).

demonstrate that a loving attitude awaits inside, making a home's exterior entryway inviting.

I enjoy changing welcome mats and door wreaths for each season. They lend a gracious greeting to your family and guests. We (and most guests) enter through our back door so I replace them often due to the wear and tear from weather and deck travel. When selecting a welcome mat, choose one that suits your style and the message you would like conveyed to visitors.

While clean and orderly entrances are important, it is even more important that each guest to our home senses a spirit of comfort and hope. We often have people in crisis or pain stop by for counsel. A friendly entrance puts others at ease before ever opening the door. A visual invitation of "welcome" takes very little effort, but can make a big difference.

Take time to stand outside and take a look at your front door. Walk up to it. See and feel what guests see and feel. Maybe it's time to give it a lovely new color that stands out or new brass hardware that glows with greeting!

Most of all, you yourself can become a door of *hope* to all who enter your life. Throughout Scripture, God is referred to as our spiritual safety, security, and source of comfort. We are to run to Him for rest from the storms and stresses of life. He totally accepts you. He loves you with an everlasting love. He is your refuge. He is constant and reliable . . . always there. With Him we will never know the meaning of the term "homeless" because He promises, "Never will I leave you nor forsake you" (Heb. 13:5).

Too often we believe the lie, "This is hopeless." Maybe you are really hurting and suffering today or bearing deep pains from the past . . . and the last thing on your mind is giving your front door a makeover. In fact, like many women I've met, your real fantasy is to throw in the towel and put a FOR SALE sign out in front of your house. My heart goes out to you today.

I want you to know that there *is* hope. To the extent that you will throw open wide the door of hope and walk in, you will find healing and comfort. God will transform your "Valley of Achor" (trouble) into a door of hope! (see Hos. 2:15). What a glorious promise! In the same way our hearts turn toward home for a physical refuge, we can turn to Him for comfort . . . and then begin to redecorate from the ground up!

Believe me, I know.

Dirty Windows in My Pain

One chilly fall day, I remember sitting in the living room of our

Walton-style farmhouse. This was almost 20 years ago. I was not quite 30 years old, but felt 90. Looking out at the autumn wonderland sent a bittersweet ache to my heart. The world outside was so lovely, but I didn't know where or how I fit in to the world inside of me.

Sitting for hours on that sofa, I asked myself for perhaps the first time, "Who am I? Why am I here? Where am I really going?" I dared not know who the real me really was. I longed to know but was afraid of finding out. I had become a slave to what the "they" in my world would think. So used to playing the role according to what others wanted for me, *I* didn't even enjoy being around me — how could I expect my friends and family to?

So I just sat in my living room. And sat. When Rob would come home at noon I would be in the same robe, in the same chair, watching the same TV channel. It was just too much effort to get up, walk across the room and change it. (This was back in the year B.R.- Before Remote.)

I'd sit and stare out the windows. Windows, that in previous fall seasons I would have enjoyed cleaning to a bright shine. Not that fall. Like the clouded spirit inside of me, the windows of our home became more and more difficult to see clearly through. I didn't know if they would ever come clean. As the weeks passed, I didn't even care.

Existing, Not Living

Have you, too, had a difficult time putting comfort in your home because you have not met the first prerequisite: a healthy attitude and acceptance of yourself? Comfort in your own heart is necessary before there can be a comforting attitude toward others. Like I was for so long, maybe you have been unable to be positive, honest, and comfortable being the *real* you.

Unable to develop my own personality and talents, frustration mounted. I stooped to be a copy of someone else rather than accept that God made me an original. My thinking had become distorted. I blamed everyone else for my pain and problems. For a long time I wallowed in the mire of self-pity, thinking I was destined to be miserable. Life was passing me by. I was existing, but not really living.

Conscious efforts by well-meaning friends and family to "fix Sharon" were to no avail. Everyone who knew me commented on how poorly I looked and asked if I was feeling all right. I'd be a wealthy woman today if I had a dime for every time I was asked that year, "Are you okay?" Admittedly, I was getting scared myself. I knew the reflection in the mirror wasn't the person I was used to seeing. I forced myself through the daylight hours, grateful

Comfort in your own heart is necessary before there can be a comforting attitude toward others.

when nightfall came. At least there was one escape.

After a while, sleep ceased to be the answer. I could not sleep for more than a few hours nightly and stayed up for alarming hours at a time. Decisions became impossible to make. When I did make a choice as to what to wear for the day, I would wear that outfit the whole week — making a decision to change was more than I could get through. In Rob's sincere efforts to be an encouragement, he came home at noon one day to whisk me away for lunch. Reluctantly, I went along. The look on his face that I felt responsible for was too painful not to go.

That lunch changed the course of our next year. Staring at the menu big ol' tears began to roll down my cheeks. I couldn't decide. Rob came to my rescue by telling the waitress I did not feel well. Choosing the first thing my eyes could focus upon, I announced I'd have the chili. Bless her heart. When the waitress returned with the news that they were all out of chili, I fell apart. Now I knew I'd have to make another choice. And I knew I couldn't.

Rob knew he had to get me home. The little waitress followed us all the way to the door, apologizing all over herself for upsetting me so.

On the way home Rob held me tenderly, but talked to me firmly. He told me we were going to go for help. We didn't know exactly where to go, but we *were* going. I had come to the end of my strength and wanted help for myself as badly as he wanted it for me. Our search began the very next day. I found myself pouring out my "symptoms" to a long-time friend of ours who was a medical doctor as well as a psychologist.

I assumed he would take x-rays, run test after test on all my body parts that were hurting, write a prescription or two, and we'd be on our way. It didn't happen that way. A short exam and blood test later, this wise doctor said aloud what Rob and I had been afraid to. "Sharon is not sick, she's depressed. Clinically depressed. She needs help — more than I can give her as an out-patient." It was difficult to hear the prognosis, but with it came a remarkable sense of hope. Hope that I might finally get help!

I had not planned to spend the next weeks in a psychiatric hospital, but in that safe place I began to heal. Unresolved anger and resentment from my painful past was causing conflict in my present relationships. My years of anger turned inward resulted in deep depression. Like looking through dirty window panes, my problems didn't *cause* everything to look distorted. But, cleaning up the dirt inside of me began a whole new perspective. Then and only then, outside began to look brighter!

How Did I Get the Capacity to Comfort?

Just when I felt I was losing my mind, ultimately, God intervened and brought help. He has sent the Holy Spirit to be our Comforter (John 14:26). That's how I received peace and began to experience His soothing comfort.

Using dear family and friends as channels of His love, God began to comfort my sorrowful soul. Their kind practical deeds and quiet presence to listen brought hope. Did they quote Bible verses? Or did they try to analyze and explain away what was happening? No. I was in no state of mind for pious platitudes or haughty explanations.

Much to my surprise, I was assured by their loving care, that God's comfort could finally bring peace to my heart. God has since used our home to be a channel of His comfort to many sorrowing and hurting people. God "comforts us in all our troubles, so that we can comfort those in any trouble" (2 Cor. 1:4).

> The comfort God has given us
> He wants us now to share
> With others who are suffering
> And caught in life's despair.[1]

God comforts us to make us comforters, not to make us comfort-able. Without a basic willingness and ability to care for, love, and nurture yourself, it is very difficult to achieve a deep or lasting ability to comfort others. Taking good care of yourself is the foundation on which the pathway to comforting others rests. It is not something that develops overnight or as a result of any single insight decision. But for most of us, it is a modification in our behavior. We *build gradually* through a willingness to work on a number of areas in our life.

The Best Vitamins for Your Soul

Good emotional health is a product of meeting the nutritional needs of your soul. If you wish others who live in your home to be loving, caring, and comforting people — first *you must B-ONE!* Acknowledging and meeting your own basic human needs is a way you can learn to care for yourself.

It was not until the last few decades that physiological needs were identified as essential to life. While necessary for survival, meeting these needs is also essential to your emotional well-being and a satisfying life.

Recognize what your own needs are. How

God comforts us to make us comforters, not to make us comfortable.

many of the following do you feel are being met sufficiently in your own life?

1. Physical safety and security
2. Financial security
3. Friendships
4. Respect
5. Validation
6. Sense of belonging
7. Nurturing from others
8. Physical touching and being touched
9. Loyalty and trust
10. Sexual expression and fulfillment in marriage
11. A sense of progress of goals
12. Creativity
13. Spiritual awareness — personal relationship with your Creator-God
14. Unconditional love
15. Fun and play

Many of these needs can greatly be fulfilled right in your own home. How many of these listed needs are actually being met at this time? In what areas do you come up short or feel are mostly unmet? Learn to (1) recognize and (2) meet your basic needs as a human being. Then, and only then, you are able to care for and nurture others!

Self-nurturing Activities

By performing at least one or two items from this list or one of your own daily, you will grow in the important skill of becoming a good nurturer of yourself. You have nothing to gain except an increased esteem and positive feelings. In our world we are taught to love God and be kind to our neighbors, but somehow we have a problem with knowing how to love ourselves.

I have found that many women give and give so much to others, there is no time left for themselves. As a young wife and mother, I found I had little energy or budget left to do special things for myself. It really took its toll and I began to burn out. As I began to take a more wholesome approach to this area of caring for myself, I found more satisfaction in every area. As I speak in front of various groups, I meet many women who are discouraged and defeated from juggling their many roles in life. When they learn to care for themselves because they

Learn to recognize and meet your basic needs as a human being.

are important in God's eyes, they are much more apt to avoid burnout and defeat. We must plan time in each of our days *to care for ourselves.* Some comforting, fun ideas to get you started include:

- Take a warm bath
- Make #1 a bubble bath
- Buy that bundle of flowers you usually pass up
- Go to a zoo
- Have a manicure or pedicure
- Get up early and watch the sunrise outside
- Buy yourself something on your lunch hour
  (you can afford!)
- Swing in the park (one of my personal favorites)
- Work on a favorite puzzle
- Go to a hot tub or Jacuzzi
- Take a brisk walk listening to an affirmation tape
- Walk the beach
- Begin planning this summer's vacation
- Browse in a card, garden, gift, or book shop
- Write an encouraging card to a friend
- Rent a good film or feel-good movie
- Dawdle — take more time than you need to
  accomplish whatever chore you're doing

- Visit a museum or city landmark
- Listen to a positive, motivational tape
- Write in your journal
- Apply fragrant lotion all over your body
- Exercise
- Sit and hold your puppy
- Go to bed early
- Fix a special dinner, eat by candlelight
- Sleep out under the stars
- Take a scenic drive around a lake
- Go to a fine restaurant or tea room
      — just with yourself
- Grill out — watch the sun set

Others contribute to but cannot meet your deep needs of adequacy and confidence. Only God truly can. He has put within each of us a void that only He can fill. He is always there, patiently waiting for us to turn to — and run to — Him. When you do, joyous acceptance, respect, and validation of being *you* re-affirms and strengthens a positive attitude and feelings about yourself. God loves you, He accepts you, He sees you! Psalms 147 is an intimate love letter from your Heavenly Father confirming that!

Customized Comfort

Honoring your own needs contributes greatly to personal wellness. Daily focusing on taking care of your needs will have a direct impact on the level of comfort in your home. Four areas which involve different levels of your whole being include:

> BODY: Physical body and well-being
> FEELINGS: Your emotional self-expression
> MIND: Positive affirmations
> SOUL: Personal relationship with the Savior

Just like a fine piece of machinery, each part must run properly for us to perform as God intended. It's likened to a four-legged stool. If one leg is weak or too short, no one better try sitting on it!

Most women I know want to be capable, confident, effective, and strong. Naturally, the more you care for yourself, the more confident you will be! We sabotage comfort right in our own homes when we do not practice personal wellness. Daily. It's that simple! No matter how good your intentions may be, no woman can handle the stress of managing a home when she has not given herself vital opportunity for essential refueling.

Be creative in this area, but don't forget the obvious. I began a practice of sound mind and body habits quite out of necessity. My own negative self-talk, destructive health and sleep patterns, along with a "victim" ("poor me") attitude had begun to render me hopeless and powerless. Days of depression led to weeks, and I was gradually "stuck" — unable to move out of the doubt, fear, and despair.

Every woman I have ever known has dealt with depression to some extent. Many battle with it monthly like clockwork. Overcoming the problem is never a singular task. I had to learn to rely on family and a very godly friend-counselor whom I respected. Through very small steps at first, we developed a plan of action to find my way out of the numbed-out emotional state.

I then had a "map" to follow. Not groping in darkness any longer, I began to see rays of light. Fear finally diminished. Hope returned! To this day, I still refer to the "map" when I get stuck on obstacles along life's way.

Too Pooped to Ponder?

By far, the foundational starting point on that map to achieving peace is *setting an actual appointment with God every day.* I have found that setting a specific appointment time (the night before) to

God has put within each of us a void that only He can fill.

meet with God really helps me stay committed. If one of us is not there, guess who is the "no show"? I don't dare stand up the Lord! I need to settle my heart with God before the day begins with its constant interruptions, phone calls, and unexpected surprises. He, too, longs to fellowship with me!

Start small so you won't get overwhelmed and discouraged. Choose a specific amount of time that will be your set appointment time. This used to sound unappealing to me, but I found that I need the structure — it increases the probability of my actually keeping my appointment.

We could all give up 15 minutes a day of sleep or another activity in order to slip away (you'll find yourself slipping in more time many days!). A sense of direction, a plan, can make the difference between a home of comfort and just surviving the day! To generate peace in my own heart that will eventually carry over into relationships, I must first meet with the Prince of Peace. "My peace I give to you," He promises (John 14:27).

Keeping your appointment daily with your Heavenly Father will have a direct impact on your home's comfort level, as well as contribute substantially to your own well-being. Spend that time reading His love letter to you, His Word. Come away nurtured, cherished, ready to face the day because you have laid it out before the Lord. You're cultivating a relationship with the Lord of the universe. That is truly astounding.

Meet Him with an attitude of anticipation. Imagine Him sitting across the table or with you on your sofa. He is a personal God. He is not some unfamiliar, distant stranger that we awkwardly approach in fear and trembling. As you spend time with Him and His words spend time in you, you will enjoy the intimacy of the closest of relationships.

Practice Makes Perfect

It's like any discipline. In order to follow through with a personal commitment, we must structure in a time block. I actually put my "morning watch," as Andrew Murray called his time with God, right in my day-timer. Otherwise, my time with God dwindles down to no time with God at all.

Build in variety, set times, regular evaluation, goals, and the proper tools: non-distracting setting . . . Bible . . . journal . . . autobiographies of great men and women of the faith. You are cultivating a relationship with the Lord of the universe. Holding a conversation with Him, sharing your hopes, dreams, and affections, listening to His affections for you . . . that's a daily appointment you can't miss!

I find that the combination of *daily prayer and Bible reading* has made it much more natural for me to make running to God my first response when in the midst of uncontrollable circumstances. I'm reminded that nothing — not death nor life, nor principalities, nor languid prayer and half-hearted Bible study — will be able to separate me from God's constant and abiding love.

"I will not forget you! See, I have engraved you on the palms of my hands" (Is. 49:15-16).

When I stand to sing a solo, I jot the first few words of the song on my hand just to get me going. God has engraved us on his loving palms!

God's Word is always timely and comforting! My Bible is splashed with underlined verse and ink marks next to verses of hope during times I need a lift. That is why it is so important to develop one's own regular Bible-reading plan. Always timely and comforting, we can run to Him — for His promises are there to catch us during any fall.

Your Dream Home

What a way to bring comfort to your home . . . from the inside out! It is impossible to over-emphasize the immense need humans have for security. Comfort brings that reassurance; you feel safe and protected from the storms of life. The beautiful thing is that the more secure we feel in our home life, the more confidence we have to live life beyond the walls of our home.

The door to comfort is really there waiting for any of us to open and go through.

What does it take to find comfort at your own address? Several things. Rare, beautiful qualities in a woman. Like time. Hugs. Listening. Care. Unselfishness. Encouragement. Laughter. And perhaps, most of all, letting yourself rest securely and comfortably in the hands of God.

> A house is made of
> walls and beams,
> A home is built with
> love and dreams.

I have engraved you on the palms of my hands

(Is. 49:16).

When Your Home Is Falling Apart

Whatever else might be said about home, it is the number one place where I long to be when I have been on the road traveling very long. I've seen and been to some awesome places and am very blessed to have met some wonderful friends away from my home. The plain and simple truth remains as accurate today as the day Dorothy said it in "The Wizard of Oz": "There's no place like home!"

When I've been gone "flying the friendly skies" for very long, my own bed and warm fireplace feels pretty good. Be it ever so humble, there's just no place like it! Recently, I returned after a week-long exhausting ministry trip to find flowers blooming everywhere that hadn't even budded when I left. What a welcome! Grabbing my camera, I ran out to the front of the house and snapped a picture. I felt like Jimmy Stewart as he raced throughout his house after the realization of what home truly meant to him. "I love you, you old house!" he cried . . . broken banister railing and all!

Chaos. Yes. I returned to my home's comforts, but also to its concerns. So much for the photo opportunity. The very next day, real life rushed in. I wanted to cry. I began to understand what I read the other day on a bumper sticker. It read: "Life is like ice cream. Just when you think you have it licked, it drops all over you."

My morning started out like the recitation of "You know you're going to have a bad day when. . . ." First, I put both contacts in ONE eye. Then hurriedly, I began to make the first of eight calls I needed to return, each one to hurting people that took longer than usual to counsel. On to the long distance calls — only to discover our long distance service was down temporarily. Groan. All morning I kept looking for just a little encouragement, some small joy.

But, that day it seemed as if finding joy was not going to be an easy thing to do. I was already way behind by noon, but headed out to run errands anyway.

The cleaners had lost Rob's favorite shirt. I managed grocery shopping (yes, my cart had those wheels on it that go in every direction). Having misplaced my grocery list, this stop took twice as long trying to shop by memory. (I just knew I'd brought that sticky note with me.) The kind gentlemen behind me in the line found it for me . . . right on the seat of my pants! To top it off, going through the fast food drive-up lane for my chicken salad, the wooden railing reached out and grabbed the entire length of the car. Rob's car. Rob's brand-new, two-week-old car!

Life is like ice cream. Just when you think you have it licked, it drops all over you.

Frazzled, Frustrated, and Frantic

With tears having ruined my mascara and my best-laid plans scrapped, I returned home wondering how the day could ever be salvaged. Life and its upsets seemed to be gaining momentum. By the end of that day, everything I'd tried to accomplish was in chaos and I was frazzled, frustrated, and frantic!

What a blessing when my eye caught sight of a visible reminder of how special I am to God. It was the shiny Red Plate in my china hutch on which is engraved: "You are special today!" I'm sure you have heard of these plates and may even have one yourself. They are designed after a custom among early American families. When some-

one in our home deserves special praise or attention, our custom is to serve their meal on the special plate.

Oh, how I needed this reminder right then! Its message caused me to remember that today and *every day* I am special to God. It just seemed to wrap me in the comfort of God's love. Even if it isn't my birthday, or Mother's Day, or when I've accomplished something outstanding, God's love is still the same *every day*.

With tears welling up in my eyes I paused to drink in the Red Plate's message.

Not much else seemed to go right in our home that entire week. I made a point to pause often in front of our Red Plate to let God's comfort blanket wrap around me again and again. I truly believe God cares for us and uses even the smallest of things to reveal His love.

I know there are a lot of bigger problems in the world, but mine had piled up so high that I could not see past them. I want to remind you of how special you are today — to me and to God — you ARE a Somebody! How I wish I could reach out to everyone hurting right now and serve each one of you a lovely meal on your very own shiny Red Plate. As I've had to at the close of many a growly day, you can get a fresh start. Accept what you cannot change, and with God's help, put the past behind you. You can, if you will:

TRACE IT! — Trace your problem to the root of your pain. You might be shocked to find out that what you are allowing to dominate your life is not the real problem at all. Until I got a grasp on the pain of insecurities from abandonment in my young years, I could not trust others, God, or my husband. I assumed they would not be there for me someday but would leave me abandoned. When I traced fears that had been embedded for so long, I could then escape from them. And, more importantly, move on! Past pain does not have to have a grasp on every aspect of your life.

FACE IT! — Take positive action steps to amend, forgive, then remove whatever it is that paralyzes you with heartache and fear. It is much easier to submit to emotional surgery for removal of the turmoil, than to let the harmful disease fester forever, infect, and eventually inflame every area of your life.

ERASE IT! Surrender your "it" to the Lord and He will wipe the slate clean with His special eraser called FORGIVENESS. What is "it" that holds you captive? You cannot conquer pain, injury, suffering, and anxiety in your own strength. Only God can truly set us free . . . remarkably free from even the memory of your pain! There isn't any situation so bad that it can't be forgiven. Keeping your "it" bottled up inside will only make you bitter. First, we must relinquish. Give your pain away. No more rehashing and reviewing . . . it is no more. Where once you felt pain's icy fingers, God will hold you in His everlasting arms.

"I sought the Lord, [TRACE IT!] and he answered me; [FACE IT!] he delivered me [ERASE IT!] from all my fears" (Ps. 34:4)

The Best Security System You Can Install

Dear Reader, your life's predicament may be full of "unexpecteds" such as the day I just described, or there may be blows more severe than you can bear. Losses, calamitous illness, release from a job, sudden death . . . your home may be falling apart. If you are not experiencing a trial today, hold on! You will be soon! That's life! Scripture tells us that we will not escape trouble and to not think it strange when fiery trials come upon us (Ps. 34 and James 4). There will come a time when your faith is severely tested. Remember, life is not fair. But, God is!

A Home Built to Last

May I carefully share a biblical principle that will uphold and sustain you in a day of trouble. The bedrock, incredible truth is: *When everything or everyone else seems against you, God is for you!*

What wonderful good news! That God is FOR us, not against us (Rom. 8:31). I can think of nothing more assuring and securing. He really is a God I can trust. He's shown me time and time again by what He has done in my own home in the face of pain, doubt, and despair. I've seen God prove himself over and over.

Storms come, winds blow, and the rains descend upon all of our homes. Both houses described in Matthew 7 were rained upon, indicating that no home is exempt from storms. Life just seems to go

He will wipe the slate clean with His special eraser called forgiveness.

from one extreme to another. The foolish builder hurries, putting materials together in a "hodgepodge" way. Here . . . there . . . whatever is available at the time or easiest. When the rains come, that house falls.

I can remember singing the chorus about the foolish man who "built his house upon the sand." I loved when we came to the part, "And the house on the sand went SPLAT!" We'd give a big clap and fall down out of our seats.

But . . . the wise man built his house upon the rock. Yes, his faith was under attack outside the four walls of his home. He had to constantly fight against the onslaught of the world's philosophies that stormed down upon his rooftop. The song chants, "And the house on the rock STOOD FAST!" It did not fall because its foundation was Jesus Christ, the rock.

"Lord, You are my rock and my fortress and my deliverer; my God, my rock, in whom I take refuge" (Ps. 18:2, Deut. 32:4, Ps. 27:5).

Talk about home security — a home built on Jesus Christ will last! Even when the floods come, as they did in our home here in Des Moines in 1993. Our family experienced great loss of the entire downstairs level of our home during statewide flooding. Many of our personal belongings, pictures, Christmas decorations, clothing, and household items were ruined. I grieved at the sight of these material possessions as they lay six days in separate piles until the insurance adjuster could get to our home.

These losses hurt deeply, especially the sentimental items that could never be replaced. But, our true home, that which is in the hearts of Rob, Sharon, Missy, and Mindy, that love withstood the flood waters. Our home had been built upon the rock — we stood secure.

Homing Instinct

No person, event, or circumstance can thwart God's good plan for your life because He is for you. Even when everything seems to work against you. Jeremiah 29:11 promises, "For I know the plans I have for you . . . plans to give you hope and a future." You can stop nailing yourself to a cross because Jesus was nailed to one for you. You can live a guilt-free life from here on out! When we do sin, we have an advocate with God, the Father — His Son, Jesus Christ. That's why you can keep coming to God for complete forgiveness. No, you cannot change the past, but you can get full forgiveness for what happened in the past (see 1 John 1:9, 2:1). That hope is better home improvement than any restoration job you can tackle.

For I know the plans that I have for you

(Jer. 29:11).

What are you a captive of? Name it, then turn yourself over to God, surrendering all, and He will set you free! Trust in His love and character. Joy will return! I had let Rob down. But, you see, I trust Rob profoundly. I trust in his love and his character enough to know that he wants the best for me. I know that his love goes deeper than my scratching his car. Trusting someone means you risk. You risk being let down, betrayed, or hurt.

Perhaps that's why the trust of a little child is so precious. A small child trusts that we will catch them when they jump into our arms. They just jump! In their child-like vulnerability they trust. Unfortunately, these days we have to teach them that you can't just trust anybody. "You could be hurt, cheated, even murdered," we're forced to warn.

You know what it's like to be betrayed by someone you trusted. I can still feel the hurt, disappointment, and fear I felt as a young child spending my first few years in inconsistency. My mother had contracted tuberculosis when it was rampant in the fifties, shortly after I was born. For some months doctors sent her for therapy and rest at a sanitarium in a nearby city.

I knew that my mother loved me, but I couldn't trust her at t when I felt like separation was abandonment and rejection.

I was sent from one relative or church member's house to another, since my daddy pastored a new, struggling work and could not feasibly take care of my sister and me at such young ages. No one was able to keep us very long. After all, they had their families and lives to lead. So we spent a short while at each willing person's home, then were moved on. I thought it was me. I thought no one wanted me. I must have been in the way, too much trouble.

Finally we were back together as a family. But, the consistency did not last very long, My lack of trust deepened. My mother got sick again, this time with polio. I couldn't even trust her to go on living. Mother died when I was just three. To a child, the death of a parent is the ultimate betrayal. Even though my daddy did the best he knew to help my sister and I feel secure, we had lost the security that only a mother can bring to a child. I felt abandoned.

I didn't know how to grieve. In fact, I was playing "funeral" with my dolls in shoe boxes the day after Mother was buried. It wasn't until many years later that I was guided to grieve the loss and begin the long journey of learning to trust. Placing a rose at her grave with my dear daddy standing at my side began the healing process — for which I am eternally grateful. Then and only then, was I able to begin loving and trusting the dear mother God had given us as a gift from Him.

No, my situation did not change. I chose to forgive my mother for dying. After all, it was not her choice. It happened. My attempts to discern or understand were futile. But, my choice to accept changed everything! When my trust factor was restored, I could trust God as well. After all, He is for me, not against me (see Is. 43:1-3 and Ps. 119:6).

I can trust God because of what He is and because of what He has done. He has shown me who He is and proven many, many times that He is trustworthy. To me the most incredible part is that He will never abandon me or reject me. I am loved and redeemed by God; His Word tells me so. Perhaps the greatest theology I've ever learned is in the little Sunday school chorus, "Jesus loves me this I know, for the Bible tells me so."

God really is a parent I can trust. He's shown me His trustworthiness by what He has done in my life and in the lives of so many people I know. I think of so many people — young moms, single parents, parents looking for their prodigals, men and women with life-threatening illnesses. They are an example for me of God's care in their weakness and pain. He will do the same for you! God has given you all you need to confidently trust Him. In His Word we're promised:

• His presence: "I will never leave you nor forsake you" (Josh. 1:5).

• His provision: "I was young and now I am old, yet I have never seen the righteous forsaken or their children begging bread" (Ps. 37:25).

• His protection: "The Lord is my light and my salvation. . . . The Lord is the strength of my life; of whom shall I be afraid?" (Ps. 27:1;KJV).

Trust is the antithesis of fear. This is a God who has given me the assurance of His presence when I give Him my trust. When I look back at the way my life has unfolded, I stand astonished at the goodness and mercy He shows. He is constantly releasing streams of blessings my way! To this woman who distrusted everyone and had good reason to, He has healed that distrust by giving me a new mother, a faithful daddy, and a strong, dependable, nurturing husband whom I am able to trust without reservation.

This same trustworthy God transformed a

Jesus loves me this I know, for the Bible tells me so.

willing but inexperienced young wife and put her in ministry with her best friend. Then, He gave her the opportunity to teach others what she has learned through a nationwide ministry of writing and speaking. My cup runneth over!

How about you? Are you having a hard time trusting . . . trusting God . . . or your husband . . . or those in your past? God is able to run this universe and He certainly is capable of taking all the pain and fears in your heart and turning them into "exceedingly abundantly more than you can ask or think" (Eph. 3:20). His goodness, even in the most painful hour, pursues you to comfort and settle you.

What to Do When Your House Is Falling Apart

I think of my friend Denise Chapman. No, her house didn't blow down or fall down, but the very foundation was shaken two years ago. She was making her weekly jaunt to Wal-Mart like so many of us American women do. Having a little extra time this day, she allowed her two year old the privilege of riding the merry-go-round in front of the store. Tenderly she placed the baby carrier with six-month-old Nathaniel resting quietly inside on the pavement beside her foot. Turning to place the quarters in the machine, she watched Jonathan smile as he anticipated the ride.

In split-second timing Denise heard the loudest noise she's ever heard coming from behind her. She caught sight of the car speeding toward and crashing into the wall of Wal-Mart, carrying with it the precious cargo of Nathaniel in his carrier. At the same time the car, whose accelerator had stuck, brushed across Jonathan's leg, severing it just above the kneecap.

I can't even begin to describe the agony of this young family's loss. Nathaniel was killed instantly. Jonathan, now two years later, plays as happily as any other little fella — when he gets tired of his prosthesis, he just removes it and props it up in the corner awhile. The trust in God's sovereignty is a dramatic witness to God's trustworthiness. He has been this home's firm rock, a sure foundation. He has proven to be their door, their way, truth, and life, their secure rock upon which to stand — even on days they feel like they are going to fall.

I wondered how they would ever learn to function in joy again. But, they have! What a privilege it has been to see God provide through the past two years. He has been with them through their pain, and now through their gains. In January of this year, God blessed them with little Hannah. Even her name is a tribute to God's reliability.

There is not a time that I enter a Wal-Mart now that my eye does not catch sight of the yellow posts that are protective barriers so that such a tragedy might never happen again. Nor is there a time that I do not pause to praise God for His constant reminders in our lives that He can be trusted. Then I pause to ask His special sweetness to be upon Denise's family that day.

Take a look at the word "sovereign." Underline the last five letters. R-E-1-G-N. Without letting God reign "supremely, above all others," as Webster's says of the meaning of the word, we are doing the reigning, not Him. We must give Him the reins, if you will, to reign!

As a result of trusting, my life is much more peaceful. He knew what was best all the time. Oh, sometimes I think I do, but God has a clearer sense of the beginning AND the end. That's why I must trust as an act of my free will. It forces me to grow. There's no place I can go that He will not be with me. There are still times my pain of living in uncertain homes my first few years of life wraps over me like a blanket of betrayal.

Do I have to run back to my Heavenly Father for my comfort?

Of course, I do. Every single day.

The master architect lovingly restores — putting more security into our home than any infrared sensor mounted to a transmitter that beams up to 100 feet away!

And there are no batteries needed. Just complete childlike trust.

My Very Scary Hall Closet

Not so long ago as our guests stood to leave, all I remember Rob saying was, "Let me get you an umbrella. It's really pouring out!" Then he turned to me to find out exactly where the umbrellas were. I was busted. Ugh! That hall closet was really scary. I certainly did not want all my company seeing the dead, rotting . . . who knows what all was in there.

My intentions were good. I *meant* to get to cleaning closets. Sometime. Tomorrow. You know how it is. There are just certain places in our house that are the last to be tended to . . . and THAT closet was one of them. "That's okay," responded our guest, reading my thoughts (or the look of sheer panic on my face). I watched them start out the door in the pouring rain . . . vowing to clean closets tomorrow!

The very next day humiliation drove me to tackle cleaning the hall closet first. It WAS scary! Winter coats, gloves and scarves, tennis rackets, extra coffee maker — to name a few of the treasures I found. The first thing I did was take everything OUT. Then I cleaned, even painted, and

There's no place I can go that He will not be with me.

placed only the useful necessities back inside. The whole hallway smelled fresh when we walked by.

One closet led to another. After inventorying each room, I cleaned closet by closet with each family member in tow. We added some super wardrobe organizers and were amazed at the space they provided. Re-organizing clothes by putting three boxes nearby worked well for us. One box was marked "to give to friends," one box marked "Salvation Army," one box marked "seasonal." We all now rotate seasonal clothing between the storage room and bedroom closets to provide better organization and more space.

If you do not have adequate storage space, purchase inexpensive

standing or hanging wardrobe "closets" for easy alternating of seasons. We wrote "summer" and "winter" on the lids of storage boxes, as well, and just turn the lid around for whichever season is applicable for sweaters and other stored folded clothing.

I like what Emile Barnes has for a closet motto: "When something new comes in, something old goes out . . . too many is too many!" When we purchase or receive gifts of underwear, ties,

nighties, shoes, etc. — when the new one goes in, an old one goes out!
Simplify . . . simplify . . . simplify. Saves space and clutter!

Clutter-Free Closets

Are you using all your closet space? How about storage boxes on
the top shelf, more rods and hooks for the children's rooms? Shoe trees?
And if you can, buy padded hangers for dress wear and plastic ones for
sports wear. Give all those wire ones back to the cleaners.

Is everything within reach, or are you having to make a lot of
steps when dressing? Maybe the furniture needs re-arranging for more
convenience. Important note: if you live with a husband, be sure he has
ample space for organization and dressing. Many times women are
concerned about their needs in "their home." Consideration for your
husband's needs will show him silently how important he is to you.

Maybe you want to go all out and re-paper your closet with per-
fumed paper, with matching paper and ribbon and border for shelves
and shoe boxes. You know how far and how creative you want to go in
this area. The ideas are endless. I find that when I have something
decorated I tend to keep it better organized.

If you haven't worn items in your closet in a year, why haven't
you? Too loose, too tight? That's another whole area you need to lay
out before the Lord and discuss with your doctor. There are so many
books on the subject of proper weight control. A wonderful one that

friends of mine use is called "First Place." It contains terrific practical, medical, and spiritual guidance for submitting the control of your weight and healthy eating to the Lord. And I'm just as emphatic about encouraging its use for the worrier, anorexic, or bulimic woman who's too thin! No problem is too big for God. He wants you to be a radiant picture and healthy advertisement of His care for His own.

Now step back from your closet. Is there a nearby full-length mirror? Is there a place for everything and everything in its place? Is there adequate lighting? Or are you like I was and couldn't tell the navy from the black pump? Yep, I did wear one of each to church, and yes, it was the Sunday I was to sing a solo!

Whoa! I should have cleaned my closets sooner. But, with great satisfaction, I stood back, stretched my arms and said, "Well done. No one else may know, but I know that the hidden parts of my home are clean!" What a comforting feeling. I like being clean from the inside out.

Cleaning All My Heart's Closets

I draw comfort today knowing that God will cleanse and entirely clean all the "closets" of my heart as well. No matter what junk I have stored — failures, unkindnesses of others that hurt so much, memories that won't go away, regrets, putrefying sins — I know He cares.

When I allow Jesus to open my heart's door, I can give you my word — there's no better closet cleaning! Even when I get all tied up in theological knots over the meaning of the word, Jesus *still forgives*, cleans, and washes me as white as snow.

Have you cleaned your closets of the past? I mean, really let Christ clean and move on? Paul encourages us in Philippians as he wrote of reaching forward to what lies ahead. He says to forget the past! Perhaps today many of your joy-stealers are memories that continue to haunt your mind. Why in the world do we keep bringing them up? Paul's analogy is clear. In this race called life, we are to face forward like a runner, not backward (Phil. 3:7-9).

The Power of a Flower

The day Rob returned home to find radical changes in our closets, he also found me a changed woman! "You sure are happy . . . you're like a time-release capsule ready to explode!" And explode I did . . . as I took him room by room to view my day's work on closets. In each room I received vocal bouquets of praise. It may sound silly, but Rob's

When something new comes in — something old must go out!

words rang in my ears for the next few days.

Here I was, just performing an ordinary, menial task that met the needs of our family. I wasn't expecting recognition or glory. But this simple mundane act of service seemed to demonstrate to my husband an expression of my love. Rob filled my cup to overflowing with praise. His words spurred me on to show even more acceptance and appreciation for our home.

I hope I'm learning to do that. Ladies, taking care of and adding special comfort touches to our homes shows that we are content with what we have and where we are. Discontent with our homes and possessions often indicates a self-centered attitude which leads to malicious feelings. So often wives tend to take their homes for granted and begin losing their attitude of gratitude.

I know one such woman. She relayed her story to me at one of my women's conferences. Here was a woman who "had it all" — nice home with ocean view . . . handsome provider for a husband . . . polite children who appeared to have just stepped out of a magazine. But, this young wife looked well beyond her 35 years of age. "I had the attitude 'Who needs him?'" she told me tearfully. "But, now I realize how terrible I'd feel if he treated me the way I've treated him. Our marriage is in trouble. Do you think it's too late?"

No . . . no, I don't! Appreciation and praise motivate! That principle of human nature is as old as the hills, yet we all need to be reminded again and again.

Previously, I mentioned the cheery touch that flowers bring to a home. Even more powerful is the thankful heart which does more to keep a home healthy than any other attitude in life. I have marveled at the lack of sensitivity in some relationships. Like the couple we were with at an out-of-town meeting recently. See if you've been there, too.

Me and My Ego

When the dinner arrived at our table I watched as the wife pushed aside her plate. "Oh, ick!" With utter disdain she began her cutting speech (I could tell it had been given many times before) about who was to "blame" for this poor steak. The restaurant, cook, or the cow . . . or her husband for choosing the place? I sat squirming uncomfortably, wondering why "fixing blame" was even necessary.

The evening ended with never a word of thanks or even a hint of appreciation for being treated to such a lovely place. I'm sure he will not invite her to do so again soon!

A man has a deep need in his nature to GIVE to and provide for those he loves. He finds great joy in seeing your positive response, excitement, and thanks. With thanks and gratitude, he will give and give to the best of his ability. Without it, he stops giving and misses out on having that need of human nature fulfilled.

Until I learned this truth I failed to express appreciation for what Rob did, even if I did not like the gift. One night Rob excitedly leaped in the front door waving some tickets in his hand, yelling, "I got some! I got some! Two tickets to Saturday night's gospel concert! They've been sold out for weeks! Now we get to go!"

My expression alone was enough to put out his enthusiastic fire. I made sure he could tell I was completely unimpressed. I blurted out a comment about going anyway, but I thought he knew after all these years that I didn't like that singing group! He wilted on the spot.

We went to the concert . . . and a good time was had by all. NOT.

I had committed the ultimate turnoff. Reluctant to be excited about something that meant a lot to Rob, I was unreasonable. After all, we do a lot of things that are my ideas. I'd become a taker, not a giver. So I put down my pride and asked Rob for forgiveness. I ended up having a great time at the concert . . . because I chose to! There were a lot of people there we knew and hadn't seen in a while whom I enjoyed seeing. The concert actually ministered to and encouraged my heart more than I dreamed possible.

"Giving is often misunderstood as giving up something, being deprived of, sacrificing," writes Erich Fromm in *The Art of Loving*.

Instead, he describes giving as the "highest expression of potency." "In the very act of giving," he writes, "I experience my strength, my wealth, my power. Giving is more joyous than receiving, not because it is a deprivation, but in the act of giving lies the expression of my aliveness."[2]

It was Helen Keller who said, "Life is an exciting business and most exciting when it is lived for *others.*" Keeping that thought in mind we can pray from a heart of sincerity:

> Lord, help me to live from day to day
> So that even when I kneel to pray,
> My prayer will be for *others.*
> (Source unknown)

Giving Comforts

If we lost everything tomorrow, Rob and I would love being together and starting all over again and getting to this same point the second time around! Giving to someone you love does not make a woman subservient. Submission is not subservience. That

Life is an exciting business, and most exciting when it is lived for others.

— Helen Keller

denotes involuntary action; giving is voluntary. When I give out of love or "give in" voluntarily, I am adapting. That is not being a doormat.

The principle of submission is not my original idea; I personally don't even like the idea at times. But, I do know that when I submit as admonished in Scripture, I am giving and adapting by choice. I find that my husband is not unreasonable. In fact, frequently he changes his mind and does exactly what I wanted to do all along.

When I choose to accept Rob's plan, it's my decision. I must admit, however, that when I first learned "submission" in the Bible, I misunderstood it to mean "against my will." Many women mis-read it that way. They think their husband might become a dictator and walk all over them. That's never happened once in my marriage. In fact, the opposite.

You ask, "Isn't one-sided giving unfair? How come I have to do the submitting?" The apostle Peter had something to say about this. He said: "Wives . . . be submissive to your husbands so that, if any of them do not believe the word, they may be won over without words by the behavior of their wives" (1 Pet. 3:1). This is not an easy assignment. But, the responsibility is clearly upon the wife, not the husband.

To live a life that will challenge him to make his own decision, wives must manifest a spirit of meekness and submission. He does not see that in the world or perhaps in you before making such a conscious determination. That's why the impact is so great. This cannot be done by nagging or lecturing, but by submission. A "me Tarzan, you Jane" attitude? Nonsense! A mature, adult, loving, sharing, mutually submitting attitude is what the Bible teaches (Phil 2:3-5, 1 Pet. 3:7).

A giving woman's beauty is unfading and never more evident, according to 1 Peter 3:1-4. The description there is that she is of great worth in God's sight! Once I took the first step in an effort to adapt to Rob, to my wonderment, he became an incredibly responsible husband! Submitting is not giving for the sake of getting; that is manipulation. But, I'm continually amazed to see how my own cup overflows when I fill Rob's first!

A Place Where Christ Lives

There is a story told of a wealthy man who purchased a famous picture of Jesus for a very high price. With its ornate frame and beautiful coloring, he sought to hang it in a

prominent place in his home. Finally, out of desperation, he called an interior designer. After careful examination of the house and painting, the designer said, "You just cannot make this picture fit into your house! You must make the home fit the picture."

Just so, we must each make our lives "fit" a testimony of a healthy, stable, peaceful, loving home . . . a family centered home where there is a sense of solidarity and mutual respect . . . a home where the family does things together and has a fun time doing them.

If we have invited Christ into our lives, it goes without saying that we should invite Him into our homes. Logically then, if our life is new, shouldn't our home be also?

If Jesus came to your house to spend a day or two . . .
I wonder what you'd do?
Oh, I know you'd give your nicest room to such an honored guest.
And all the food you'd serve to Him would be the very best,
And you'd keep assuring Him you are glad to have Him there.
But, when you saw Him coming, would you meet Him at the door?
With arms outstretched in welcome to our heavenly visitor?
Or hide some magazines and put the Bible where they'd been?
Would you hide your worldly music and put a hymn book out?
Could you let Jesus walk right in, or would you rush about?
It might be interesting to know the things that you would do,
If Jesus came in person to spend some time with you.
— Author Unknown (abridged)

Retreats for Rest, Restoration, and Romance

With enough stimulation in the world today, I really need my bedroom to be an incredible relaxing place. A place to find stillness. Tranquillity. Comfort. A place where the rest of the world just seems to melt away. Sound like a dream? Dreams can come true in your own private chambers — your cozy, comfortable bedroom.

Secluded from the clamor of constant noise, I can retreat to my bedroom . . . and close the door. My physical and inner life gets nurtured in this room. Every day begins and ends here. I leave my bedroom ready to go out to face a challenging, sometimes confusing world. For that reason I have filled our bedroom with decor of harmonious colors that gently beckons me to rest and unwind perhaps more than any other room in our home.

Before I set up my own housekeeping I listened to women as they guided me through their homes. In united agreement, they voiced their desire to spend decorating efforts and funds on every "seen" room in the house first. Consistently the bedroom received attention last. "After all, no one sees that

A bedroom needs to be a place where the rest of the world just seems to melt away.

room except my husband and me."

How sad! I vowed that when I married I would make sure to create a bedroom of beauty with indulgences as wonderful as the sweet dreams we would dream there. That has been my inspiration for all these many years. Even though my bedroom is the least likely room to be seen by guests, its four walls are the first thing Rob and I see each morning.

If you are undergoing a major home makeover, I encourage you to tackle your bedroom first. This room can become your haven when the rest of the house is in chaos. Turn your bedroom into the luxurious retreat you were meant to have. Let this chapter be your inspiration to create a place where you can escape, where the rest of the world just melts away.

A Soothing Sanctuary

My bedroom is not just *my* bedroom, to be sure. I jointly share this precious sanctuary with Rob, the love of my life. Images of our individual roots and combined heritage are visible in the bedroom we share more than anywhere else in our home. They serve as reminders to us of the strength of our union. We have surrounded ourselves with what we love. The whole room seems to smile, beckoning us to find repose from any number of intrusions.

From the pictures of those who are closest to us to the soft lighting and smooth sheets . . . our bedroom reflects both our personalities. Make sure yours does, too. As you do, you will begin to be drawn to your own bedroom to rest, rather than feel like it is another room where work awaits.

For that very reason we removed our desk and banished our television set from our bedroom. We just didn't want the intrusion of noise nor work staring at us when we are positioned for pleasure or seeking solitude.

The most important thing to remember when decorating a bedroom is that there is no right or wrong way to go about it. In this most personal room of your house, the only people you need to please are you and your mate.

Most of the fabrics I use throughout my home are mix-and-match checks, textured solids, and stripes coordinated with florals that I love. They combine to bring a soft beauty of God's creation outdoors to the indoors. In our bedroom I find that monochromatic hues and all-white linens create a soothing atmosphere. Whites also bring a sense of spaciousness to a room.

Many manufacturers take the guesswork out of decorating by packaging a variety of ready-made bed ensembles. Then you can opt to add your own personal touches of beautification that makes the room "you." Or reverse your comforter. Then, for a designer touch give your dust ruffle a layered look combining battenburg lace over a color. Echo the battenburg by adding a new pillow or two and gather battenburg as a valance over the top of colored curtains at your windows. (I easily turned a tablecloth into a valance!)

"Eclectic" Decorating Magic

Just this morning I implemented the oldest trick in the decorating rule book — start with what you have! Brand new looks can be created without adding so much as one new item or piece of furniture if you simply move things around.

By reversing the comforter on my bed, interchanging two pictures from a wall to a shelf, arranging a vase of misshapen flowers, and nudging both night stands in closer to the bed — you could probably have heard my shriek of delight next door!

In less time than it takes to make up a bed, I felt like I had invented a more pleasing look. From familiar to fabulous! You can do the same. Or if you have a newly acquired lamp, gift item, or piece of furniture, don't just deposit it in your bedroom.

Take a few moments and let those creative juices flow. See how you can dress up your same ol', same ol'. Come nightfall, you and your spouse will appreciate the alteration. Goodbye to boorrrring!

Whatever your decorating style: sleek, cottage cozy, fashionable, dramatic, formal Victorian, down-home country, or like my style — "eclectic," decorate your home with what brings *you* pleasure. I love the term "eclectic" because it encompasses a broad range of whatever brings me pleasure in decorating. When a particular color scheme, texture, and fabric combination, or piece of furniture "works," I don't have to know *why*. It just works for me!

Pillows are some of the items that "work" for me. A couple of lace pillows add a touch of romance to the casual floral comforter in our bedroom. They echo the curtains which hang adjacent to the bed. Hoffman's rule of thumb: the more throw pillows, the better (especially in the bedroom)!

Pillows are a perfect way to dress up your bed; they make it inviting and interesting. Rob must ask me at least once a week while making or stripping down the bed, "Are you sure we really need all these pillows?" I fervently answer, "YES!!!"

Just adding one or two items that satisfy the touch, feel, and sight, can make any room soothing and pleasurable.

Pillows seem to whisper to me "crawl in and find comfort" in or on my bed. Quilted shams with various shapes, sizes, and colors of throw pillows beautify the bed like nothing else can. Sometimes I simply nestle in stillness among them, letting my spirit be renewed.

It is there that often I will read or write in my journal, just enjoying the quiet for comfort to my soul. These 15 minutes provide for me an intermission in my day. With my heart nourished, my body cannot help but be notably enriched. I'm able to press on for whatever the rest of the day might bring.

The word "eclectic" by definition indicates items are chosen "from various sources." One doesn't need sets of things in matching fabrics or designs. Just adding one or two items that satisfy the touch, feel, and sight, can make any room soothing and pleasurable.

In today's home where every inch counts, bedrooms aren't just for sleeping anymore. They have evolved into retreats that combine sleeping quarters with spa-like baths. Consider using the same soothing tones, patterns, and linens in an adjoining bathroom for a coordinated look of continuity.

Right now, think about what you love to be surrounded by in your home. What puts you at rest? What makes you sigh, "Ahhh," when you see a designed bedroom in a magazine? Use those creative ideas as inspiration in your bedroom decorating.

Bedtime Beauty

Don't restrict your restful touches just to the bed itself! By all means, don't forget the candles (as essential in the bedroom as those pillows!) Always have them within reach! I have a pretty basketful of all shapes and sizes in our linen closet. They serve to scent the closet and are easy to fetch at a moment's notice.

Top off your moments of rejuvenation or "power naps" with soft music and candlelight. An adequate setting for relaxation is essential to the enjoyment of your bedroom, yet it is an element that is often overlooked. After all, shouldn't your own comfort and pleasure be as important to you as that of your guests? The answer is a resounding yes! Once you find comfort in your own life, you can face the world a more peaceful you. Everyone wins.

Customize your room with adequate lighting for the obvious getting-ready-for-the day routine. Lighting must be bright enough, of course, to match clothing and check hemlines. But, I like to put low-watt lamps on the night stands for a soft glow. Not only are they a delightful decorator's

With my heart nourished, my body cannot help but be notably enriched.

touch, but they provide light for late-night reading.

Candlelight adds a serene glow and warms the heart. I have recently added candles in various heights and widths cloistered on a mirrored tray atop my dresser. It's an idea I enjoyed in a bed-n-breakfast stay recently. Such a lovely touch of extra ambiance and atmosphere!

You can also find little hurricane covers to give your candles of any height a new look. I just love the new crystal bobeches that are appearing everywhere now in gift stores. These slip down over the tapers and give a mini-chandelier look. Yet another look is the tiny shade that slips over a brass form. I especially like their "quaintness" in florals or brass.

Tuck votives or column candles into virtually *anything* . . . don't just stick to candlesticks. I like to snap up small china plates, trays, and wooden dowels when antique shopping. They make such charming candle creations. Tassels, ribbons, and rosettes brighten the base or mid-point of any taper.

Be as versatile as the ever-changing seasons by using small pumpkins, fresh fruit, pine cones, or yule logs as candle bases. One of the favorite attractions that grace our Thanksgiving table are the hollowed-out gourds and pumpkins that hold all sizes of candles. After the holiday meal, they are fun to use as clever decorative touches in the bedroom. If you are ambitious you can spray paint the vegetables, glue colored leaves at the base, and place them throughout the house.

For an instant romantic glow to bedroom lighting, I drape a pink nightie over a small lamp that has a pink-tinted bulb. I really enjoy the warm, pleasing visual effect . . . and we all know that any woman is more beautiful by candlelight.

To keep a subdued glow if you think you are going to let yourself actually fall asleep, don't light a candle. Install recessed lighting or use the small lamp on a bed stand. Or you might make a promise to yourself like I have . . . that in my next home I will have a dimmer switch placed in the bedroom to vary the lighting overhead. (Hmm . . . we'll see!)

Suite Dreams

Suite is a wonderful word to use for your bedroom retreat. It is a "sweet" reminder that you enter here for joy and love and laughter.

Little luxuries can enhance the sweet appeal of your current bedroom without a total makeover. Remember, the less clutter, the more the room peacefully summons you to wrap yourself in comfort. Just entering the room can alter your mood. Anxiety, stress, and even anger will be assuaged by the calm atmosphere you establish.

Try picking a bright shade for walls instead of choosing white or cream. Go for a color that makes a strong statement, but has a soothing effect. Good choices are moss green, periwinkle blue, buttery yellow, or coral. If you start with a bright color (green), add one complementary color (blue) and one neutral color (white). This is a foolproof plan where you can never go wrong!

The trick to making a small room look comfy, not crowded, is sticking with mostly solid-colored linens and upholstery. I then like to add touches of simple or whimsical patterns in moderation for interest without making the room look too busy.

"Come to me, all you who are weary and burdened," He beckons. "I will give you rest," says our Lord (Matt. 11:28). Those are not just platitudes, but sound practical advice for all of us. He knows we need regular periods of rest or we will exhaust ourselves, ending up weary, sick, and sidelined.

Perhaps one of the most treasured of items in my own bedroom is a worn, yet luxurious, handmade quilt that rests folded at the foot of my bed. It was presented to me after speaking at a mother-daughter event with a quilt theme. True, its colors enhance my decorating scheme, but the quilt's truest function is to invite me to "come away for awhile."

It is especially snuggly on chilly days or cold winter nights — feels like a big, soft hug.

And it does just that. Many are the days I put it to the test! Trying to "get life together" amid each day's heavy issues is a near impossible task without time for refueling for our body and spirit.

Renewal on the run does not bring peace to the soul. In this push-a-button, microwaveable world we live in, it does one good to remember that there are still some things that cannot be fixed by the push of a button. The soul is one of those things!

Give yourself that much-needed time out. Late in the afternoon I can often be found cuddled between my bed comforter and quilt, blanketed in warmth and comfort. Even ten minutes does me wonders! I am a much "happier camper" after even a few restful moments of recline. Resting on top of the bedspread, not in between the sheets, my entire bed does not get askew. Just a quick tidying of my quilt, then I'm ready to face the rest of the day or evening's activities.

The less clutter, the more the room peacefully summons you to wrap yourself in comfort.

Home "Rest"-oration

Inestimable is the comfort provided to a home's spirit when mom and children regularly schedule a restful time-out at some point in the day. How well I can remember those days! When Missy and Mindy were preschool age, if at all possible, I arranged at least one-half hour of quiet time. We all benefited!

The practice came from watching a noticeable difference while counseling at summer camp for children. A siesta was built right into each day's schedule as a code. No rest time, then that camper was not permitted to swim or participate in sports for the rest of the day. The consequences were straightforward and fair.

I allowed Missy and Mindy to look at books, soft sing-along tapes, color forms, stickers . . . special quiet activities brought down from the closet shelf solely for this special hour in the day. Just so they stayed reclined on the bed. Children do not have to be sleeping to be resting, and clearly every child is not going to actually sleep while napping.

But, they will be resting — whether they realize it or not.

Setting the tradition is a good one for it provides a practical separation from other siblings who might be getting grouchy. Or from a mom who might be getting growly! Not long ago I read about the small fry who said, "I didn't get up on the wrong side of the bed this morning, Mommy. I just got up on the wrong side of you!"[3]

I have not met a mother of toddlers yet who could not use a break from the pressures upon her at some point in the day. It may take a week or so of you lying down with your little one reading to him, singing, or talking softly. For our family, these became priceless moments and precious memories we still share today.

If you gasp at the thought, try it before you knock it. With unflinching authority issue the idea as something "for you." It cannot be presented as a recommendation, but as a regimen. No matter how many protests your kiddoes wail, stick it out. Refuse to be drowned in the sea of whining!

Often Missy and Mindy would fall asleep on their own, even after I had told them, "You don't have to go to sleep." I would rest with them, read, or gently get up and accomplish tasks that were waiting.

I am such an advocate of this daily time of comfort for both mom and child. There is no doubt that it is easier to give in to a willful toddler than it is to implement the disciplines of life. I know! I know! It sounds easy on paper, but it is tough to apply to everyday life. I have had trouble following this advice, too. But we can at least *try* to provide what our kids need from us. If we model discipline in our own lives, our children will be much more apt to have self-control when they are grown.

I've been speaking to large groups for well over a decade. In that time I have never met a woman whom I would consider to be inwardly peaceful who doesn't carve out some quiet time for herself in virtually every day. It helps the day to be much more manageable.

I talk to women who complain they have "no time for quiet." Work out a strategy that works for you . . . sneak in moments all through the day. On the way to pick up children from daycare, pull over for a few minutes and pause before rushing in. Try spending a few moments at the close of the day walking in nature or meditating on Scripture, or simply listening to quiet rather than clicking and whining computers or fax machines.

One final reminder concerning taking a daily time-out, or rest time! My dear friend and mentor, Norma Gillming, made it a practice when her children were young to have each of her four children rest quietly for an hour daily regardless of their protests. One particular day she noticed the hour proceeded without protest, even from her rambunctious twin sons.

It seems they had schemed a way to climb out the bedroom window and escape. Grateful for a time to read, Norma had no inkling of their escapades. That is to say, until Kenny hobbled past the living room doorway with the seat of his pants full of thorns. It seems he had landed flat in a bush below the window containing sharp spines rather than the soft ground for which he was aiming!

When rest time seems to be extending just a little too long — it might be wise to take a peek to see why!

What's Under Your Covers?

"Shadrach, Meshech, and to bed we go!" I can hear my daddy saying that phrase at bedtime as if I were a seven-year-old child again. We kids knew it was time to hit the sack and loved Daddy's ingenuity in getting us to bed. Going to sleep just wouldn't have been complete without it! Bedtime routines bring sweet security to the whole family, especially for children.

Dropping off to sleep may not always be immediate, no matter how exhausted you are. Basic principles of rest include ways to nurture the soul as well as your body. God's presence is a haven for rest.

Mini-moments of meditation bring my mind back to "stay" on God.

If time does not permit actually lying down for a reprieve, I look for moments throughout my day to re-focus my heart on God. Mini-moments of meditation bring my mind back to "stay" on God. Rest follows — both in my heart *and* my body.

Right before I rise and just before dozing off at night, in the car, blow-drying my hair — they can all be times for a time of resting in Him. I love to go on long walks down our nearby country road past the cornfields and savor God's presence. I use this time to submerge in the Word. I have found the best fat-free M and M's in the world — meditation and memorization! I use these times to focus on God and to think through my life from His perspective.

First thing in the morning I like to claim a Scripture as "mine for the day." It is often from a passage I'm reading or from a perpetual calendar for that date. A phrase or a verse sticks in my mind and re-peats in my heart to apply to my life. As my heart is drawn to Christ in dependence and worship through the day, the verse often takes on a whole new meaning and application.

At the close of the day, I let the reverberant sound of Scripture echo once again in my heart. No one is able to think two thoughts at one time. Try it — you simply can't do it. Our minds are like a television set; only one channel can be viewed at a time! If our inner lives are nourished by what is lovely, our outer lives cannot help but be better.

When you lower those covers at night, lower your stress level as well. You'll find that if you catch yourself tucking problems into bed *with* you, they don't escape outside the covers. They just cover you all night long. If you think something little taken to bed won't matter . . . you've never been to bed with a mosquito under the covers!

Pillow Talk

Being in the ministry means dealing daily with the heavy issues of life. Illness, death, broken homes and marriages, wayward children, and all manner of heartaches might be at the other end of our phone line at any time of any day.

For those reasons Rob and I make it a practice to spend the last hour of the day unwinding. We find it necessary to shut out the cares of the world and let go of the day's burdens. We might read, listen to soft music while gliding on the porch swing together, or relax watching late night TV with a big bowl of popcorn between us (low-fat, of course!).

We have done this for so long now, even when we weren't empty-nesters, that when one of us is traveling the other can retreat and still feel in touch with the other. Lying on the bed to read and await the nightly ritual of a phone-in report, we still feel in sync as if we were together. When I am the absent one, I can visualize Rob in his place as we catch up long-distance on the day's events.

Late night chats are not the times to refer to which major appliance broke that day or the latest digs in an ongoing gripe session with your mother-in-law. Spending winding-down time before retiring with your family members and/or spouse helps to balance the noise and confusion that infiltrates each of our lives virtually every day.

"All night long on my bed I looked for the one my heart loves," Solomon wrote (Song of Sol. 3:1). Quietly, in the comfort of your haven, you can retreat from the world and seek to know the one you married. Listen to his heart, his dreams, his disappointments, and his fears. As you share your time and your hearts in your private retreat you will grow in love and appreciation for each other.

You can fill the bedroom not just with comfortable, interesting items and furniture but with "rare and beautiful treasures," as Proverbs 24:4 says.

In the years ahead the walls of the room you share can give back sweet memories. Memories of love instead of anger; times of joy and laughter rather than gloom and regret.

Love Nest or Ruffled Nest?

Over the years, there were often times when Rob and I needed a private place for discussion away from Missy and Mindy, regardless of their age. Our bedroom seemed the obvious choice, but really was not a good one. Hashing out discipline problems, budget differences, and family heartaches can put a pallor on your would-be love nest. We decided not to make our peaceful place of rest a place for heated, emotional, or heavy discussion.

Even the best mattress can't provide restful sleep in a war zone! A bouquet of flowers on the dresser is never enough to eradicate the lingering scent of anger and resentment before bedtime. I encourage you not to use your bedroom for weighty subjects. Your bedroom is to be a soothing sanctuary — not a conference room or an emotional baggage terminal!

If your house is small and you have nowhere else to go, try the bathroom. Kids standing outside the door calling, "I need in there!" will help you resolve matters more quickly. Or, like one lady told me, her solution is to "haul the problem out to the

Your bedroom is to be a soothing sanctuary

garage like garbage." A long walk outside is a great solution when we find ourselves really going at it tooth and toenail over painful issues.

Start over today; decide from this time on, when you must discuss difficult issues that you will go to an "away" area. Having selected a place, be it the basement, the study, garage, attic, or outside, you can determine that voices raised in hurtful words will not be uttered in the bedroom.

Perfume the Sheets

Do you have a fragrance that elicits sweet memories from your past? The sense of certain smells instantly takes me back to places in time. Maybe it's the perfume I wore when I was dating or perhaps a pleasant floral that I recall from when Carolyn and I were college roommates walking back to campus after Sunday church in the spring. Or that lazy, hazy summer smell on a humid evening that reminds me of riding a bike endlessly as a child.

Lay the groundwork for a restful sleep by sprinkling a light powder or spraying a fresh sprit of cologne on your mattress pad or sheets. My favorite is a spray I received as a gift in the Philippines. Pulling back the spread, catching a whiff . . . it carries me back to the memories of that splendid trip. It kind of reminds me of the gardenia flower that was in a special corsage that Rob gave me in college, too.

When you count the amount of hours you sleep, the bedroom is the place in your home where you actually spend the most of your time. Fragrance makes it interesting, even distinctive. I love the scent of lilacs and was thrilled at the fresh bouquet of them Rob picked for me this spring. I have found a sachet to hang in our closet that is as endearing as those fresh-picked flowers.

Now, opening my closet at the beginning and end of each day, I feel instantly tender toward Rob when I'm met with the distinctive lilac fragrance. It seems to have the same effect on him.

Vanilla is a soothing scent that sweetens your dreams, closet, or lingerie drawers. Bedding is the perfect place to add those little touches of scented oils for sumptuous and soothing sleep.

Rest well, my friend. Rest in the shadow of God's precious winds. Instead of counting sheep . . . you can talk to the Shepherd. So shall you then find true rest. Meditate on Him in the night watch. By simply saying "peace be still," any storm in your heart can be calmed. He will never leave you nor forsake you. Remember His words . . . and rest well.

Endnotes

1 *Daily Bread*, Radio Bible Class Ministries, Grand Rapids, MI.

2 Erich Fromm, *The Art of Loving* (New York: Harper and Row Publishers, 1974).

3 Marjorie Holmes, *As Tall as My Heart* (McLean, VA: EPM Publications, distributed by Hawthorne, 1974).

About Our Cover Artist

Kit Hevron Mahoney has over 20 years experience as an artist and design professional. She was educated at the University of Colorado, Boulder, and at the Colorado Institute of Art in Denver, where she taught drawing and graphic design for 15 years. She was president/owner of Graphic Creations, Ltd., a national greeting card company and is now part owner of Abend Gallery Fine Art in Denver, where she shows her fine art. Since 1984, her watercolor and pastel landscape and floral paintings have been marketed through a variety of galleries and by private commission. Samples of her work can be viewed at http://home.earthlink.net/~kitm.